The Big Gate

For Ruth & Jim —

Best regards
& continuing respect,

Stuly
1 April 78

The Big Gate
By Elma Stuckey

Introduction by Stephen E. Henderson

Precedent Publishing, Inc.
Chicago   1976

Copyright © 1975
Precedent Publishing, Inc.
520 North Michigan Avenue
Chicago, Illinois 60611
All rights reserved
LC: 75-12115
ISBN: 0-913750-11-5
Manufactured in U. S. A.

Acknowledgment is here made to the editors of *Black Lines, Freedomways, The Journal of Black Poetry,* and *The Pan- Africanist* for permission to reprint poems first published in their pages.

Library of Congress Cataloging in Publication Data

Stuckey, Elma, 1907–
  The big gate.

  I. Title.
PS3569.T83B5   813'.5'4   75-12115
ISBN 0-913750-11-5

To my daughter and son
Jean & Sterling

Contents

xi Introduction
    by Stephen E. Henderson
1   Jim
2   Boy
3   Lettie
4   Long Cotton Row
5   No Wings
6   Burying Ground
7   The Wish
8   Driver
9   House Niggers
10 The Big Gate
21 I Been There
22 Good Masters
23 Runaway
24 Mystery
25 Shepherd
26 Hallelujah
27 Mother and Child
28 Sundown
29 Hezekiah
30 Jenny
31 Rebel
32 Mose
33 Scars and Stripes
34 Remember
35 Sissy
36 Taking Sides
37 Rebuked
38 Old King Cotton
40 Supper Time
41 Selling Melvina

42	Upstart
43	Religion
44	Duke
45	Sally
46	Tom
47	Southern Belle
48	Leora
49	Jane
50	Pete
51	Beulah
52	Family or Freedom
53	Posted
55	Telling It All
56	Mandy
57	Preacher Man
58	Tending in the Great House
59	Rain
60	Traveling Light
61	This Is It
62	Emancipation Proclamation
63	Enslaved
64	Lay Me Down
65	Movin' Nowhere
66	Cracked Saucer
67	The Vision
68	His Hands
70	Timing
71	Mourners Bench
72	An Egg in Each Basket
73	Old Man
74	Jackleg
75	Collection
76	Feeding the Pastor
77	No Flowers
78	Gambler
79	Let Them Come
80	Cannonball

81 Little Boys
82 Rigmarole: Puzzles for Children
84 Daylight Saving Time
86 New Address
87 News
88 For W. E. B. Du Bois
89 Flight
90 Uncertainty
91 Shadows in the Light
93 Trumpet

Introduction

One of the most rewarding experiences in the study and evaluation of literature is the discovery of a writer of significant talent who deserves to be better known. Elma Stuckey is such a writer. She is almost sixty-nine years old and has been writing poetry since her teens but her work, which has appeared in some half-dozen journals, is not well known.

The Big Gate, Elma Stuckey's first book of poems, is passionately felt and skillfully rendered. Like many Afro-American poets, she draws upon two traditions, the literary and the folk, both of which she handles well, but the latter with a special verve and insight which distinguish her from other writers in this vein. Her subject is no less than the revolutionary spirit implicit in the actions of the ordinary men and women who kept their humanity intact under the oppression of slavery and segregation.

The poet is the mother of Sterling Stuckey, the young historian whose seminal essay, "Through the Prism of Folklore: The Black Ethos in Slavery," in *The Massachusetts Review*, helped set the tone and direction of recent scholarship on the subject. Reading the poems, one immediately perceives the intellectual and spiritual bond between mother and son. Even more important, however, is the wider tradition, the larger continuity. These poems were *inspired* by Mrs. Stuckey's recollections of the ex-slaves in her community of North Memphis, Tennessee, where she lived until her mid-thirties. She thus serves an important role in the transmitting of this knowledge.

More important still is the distillation and interpretation of experience which her art has produced. With the exception of Dunbar, Elma Stuckey probably devotes more attention to slavery than any other poet, certainly more than any other living poet. She does not write "Dunbars," however, as poems in the tradition of Paul Lawrence Dunbar are sometimes called. She is closer in style and tone to Sterling Brown, though to be more accurate, one should say, to the realistic apprehension of the folk life and lore and art which characterizes his work. Nevertheless, the period with which she mainly deals is not the '20s and '30s of Brown's, but that of enslavement itself.

The poems in black vernacular are especially important for their variety, and for their treatment of themes current in black oral tradition but rarely set down in writing, especially in poetry. These include sexual relations between master, mistress and slave, and realistic self-portraits of black drivers, traitors, Toms, and Sambos. They include ironic and cynical attitudes toward God, as in "Long Cotton Row" and "Jim," who "got a crow for to pick with God." There is delicious humor in "Beulah," who resists her master's advances, and "Sally," with her special recipe for okra soup.

There are the common humanity and human frailty of "Emancipation Proclamation" and of "Lettie," whose "Ole Missus was as po' as me/ And both of us dipped snuff." There are lovely lyrics like "Traveling Light," and "Cracked Saucer," a commonplace object that is a quiet and moving metaphor of the human condition.

The post-slavery poems are also notable for

their variety. Some of the portraits are sharp and bluesy, as in "An Egg in Each Basket:" "Gotta stay on the good side/of the devil and with God,/Don't know which one I end up with/When they put me in the sod." Contrasted with that picture of honesty are the religious hypocrites and gulls, as in "Jackleg," "Timing" and "Feeding the Pastor," all too familiar figures of black life.

One finds among the "literary" poems the delightful word play of "Rigmarole: Puzzles for Children," the eloquent "For W. E. B. Du Bois," and the apocalyptic vision of the Last Judgment in the charging rhythm and virtuoso rhyming of "Trumpet."

Some of these poems should be read aloud, for their inner shape comes from an oral tradition which sometimes can only be suggested on the page. That is the way I first heard them: from Elma Stuckey's vital voice. Her voice comes alive in these lines. Read them and hear it. Hear it and hear the voices of the people who created the spirituals and the blues.

Stephen E. Henderson

The Big Gate

Jim

He's gonna chop his way into Heaven,
He was buried with the hoe in his hand,
And he knows just how to swing it
'cause Jim was a cotton choppin' man.

Now Jim was big and powerful,
Yeah, Jim was a six-foot man,
He's gonna chop the door wide open,
Means to get in the promised land.

Old Jim didn't say no prayers,
Bare-foot he sung them blues,
He don't like no milk and honey,
Won't wear no silvery shoes.

He swo' when he chopped the cotton,
He swo' cause he worked so hard,
Old Jim had a tough time livin',
He got a crow for to pick with God.

He's sho gonna get into Heaven,
He was buried with the hoe in his hand,
And he knows just how to swing it
'cause Jim was a cotton choppin' man.

Boy

I'se eighty year old and my name is Boy,
Ain't had no fun, but I'se had joy,
Had my joy when Marsa died,
When I moaned and wailed and laughed inside.

Lettie

Sure slavery time was rough
On our plantation, tough!
Ole Missus was as poor as me
And both of us dipped snuff.

Long Cotton Row

Lord, don't set that sun
On the long cotton row,
Look like I done chopped
'til I can't chop no mo'.

Shoo that sun over there
Right behind that cloud,
Then when breeze come 'long
I be mighty proud.

That'll make the day mo' easy,
Won't seem so long gettin' through,
And if I ain't too broken down
I'll sho be praisin' You,
That's if I ain't too broken down. . .

No Wings

I hear a wagon rumbling far away,
It's going somewhere but I'm here to stay,
Ain't got no wings so I can't fly,
If I get 'em be by-and-by

Burying Ground

One o' these days I lay cotton sack down,
I be ready for the buryin' ground.
Yeah, one o' these days I lay cotton sack down,
Go on to heaven and get my crown.

The Wish

Ole Marse has got a pointed nose,
He got a pointed chin,
Ain't got no lips but just a slit,
He look like homemade sin.

The cracks is crisscross on his neck
And he baldheaded too,
He mad 'cause he been white so long
And still ain't well-to-do.

He don't look like he human,
You can't tell front from back,
That man, he am so mis'able
I b'lieve he wish he black.

Driver

I'm glad Marse give me driver job,
It make me feel just fine,
He say to me, "You nigger you,
You keep the slaves in line."

He beat the slaves so awful,
Once that included me,
But now I beat 'em for Ole Marse,
I feel I'm just 'bout free.

House Niggers

Two times they call us from the field
And tell us Marse is dying,
Two times house niggers huddle up
And all of them is crying.

I'se sick of looking at that sight
And ask them why they cry,
They say they tired of waiting,
Marse take too long to die.

The Big Gate

*Slaves often stood out of earshot of
the master, down at the gate to the path leading
to the great house, and told
tall tales. . . .*

I

We's gathered here to tell our tales
'bout how we treat Ole Marse,
Some tales be big, some tales be small,
Sometimes the tales be sparse.

II

First of all I tell my tale.
None of you was 'round
When I pick up my fist and say,
"I'll knock you to the ground."

I say, "Old Marse, I owns you,
You knows that you is mine."
That man, he whimper like a dog,
Ain't nothin' in his spine.

Now if Ole Marse come up here
To raise hell like the dickens,
I'll chase him right between you all
And scatter you like chickens.

III

There ain't no Marse can trick me,
I'se always on the ball,
I take my fist and knock 'em dead
And don't care where they fall.

Last one I whupped, here come Miss,
She say, "Marse on the flo'!
What happen' to your Marsa?
Don't say that you don't know."

I say, "Ole Miss, I do my work
Like you done told me to,
I call you when I see him fall,
What else I s'pose to do?"

IV

I'm stuck wid Marse, he stuck wid me.
He tried to sell me twice,
The traders say, "Hell no, not Bose,
Not Bose at any price."

The secret is, I'se on the block
And so I thumbs my nose.
Marse do not see but traders see,
That's why they don't want Bose.

V

Shucks, I ain't scared o' Marse,
I treat him like a snake.
I twist his neck and stomp his tail
And curl him 'round my rake.

I talks to him like I is boss
And talk like he is slave.
If any Tom is at this gate
I put him in his grave.

VI

Ole Miss' tell Marse to beat me!
I is in puzzlement.
She knows I is de mean one,
Ain't broken and ain't bent.

I run smack-dab into dat man
And choke 'im like de devil,
Ole Missus look and clap de hands,
Say, "Boys, go git de shovel!"

VII

We s'pose to listen at this gate
But no one's heard me yet.
I got a tale to beat all tales—
Don' b'lieve me? What you bet?

I kilt Ole Marse and buried him—
You think I lie? I ain't—
If you see somethin' look like Marse
Just pay no mind, that's haint.

VIII

From miles around they knowed me,
Plantation to plantation.
I is most stubborn slave of all,
I'se hell and all damnation.

Nobody rule this brawny man,
Nobody try to whip 'im.
If S.O.B. stand up to me
I sho' to hell will lick 'im.

I'se bad, real bad, Marse knows I'se bad,
Bet you don't see 'im comin',
And if you see Ole Marse at all
You see his back, he runnin'.

IX

Look folks, pay me some 'tention
'bout what I got to say,
Y'all just so glad that Marse is dead
And buried yesterday.

Nobody ask one question,
What kilt him, made him sick?
Since you ain't ask, I shut my mouth
'bout why he died so quick.

X

I'se wishin' I could drown Ole Marse,
He plays into my hand,
Come at me when I'm fishin'
And come er-raisin' sand.

We grapple and we struggle,
We hit the river bed,
We down there where no one can see
And so I push his head.

Now that's the last I seen of him,
Don't blame no mess on me
Because I swim up to the top
And he float out to sea.

XI

Marse give us head, he give us tail
And then he give us middlins,
He give us ears, he give us feet
And then he give us chittlins.

I slip and burn the smoke house down,
Ole Marse rage and cuss,
He knowed we et the hams and ribs
that done been cooked for us.

XII

Had three Marsas in my time,
Each one was scared of me,
But being white they had to bluff
'cause other slaves would see.

They knew they could not whip me
But each just had to try,
And I done warned, "You lift that whip,
You kiss this world goodbye."

They raised the whip, I kept my word,
They never lay a lick on me,
I betcha you can find three graves
And I ain't on no tree.

XIII

Little bit of lye each day
Stirred easy in his whiskey.
Now he am in de family plot,
That way it were not risky.

XIV

Ole Marse would whup me in de field,
He says I is de lazies',
I smart 'nough to choke him good
And now he pushin' daisies.

XV

My trouble were not with Ole Marse,
It were with Marsa's Missis.
She make me climb in bed with her
And say it bettern' his is.

XVI

Hot weather come, I fan that man
'til he drop off to sleep.
I scratch my head and figure how
To make his sleep be deep.

I gather up some poison weeds
And beat them into dust,
And fan it close while he am sleep
And that am fair and just.

One night that dust hit home on him,
He did not cough or hack,
But keeled and died with crooked neck,
Doc called it heart attack.

XVII

I sing and dance for my Old Marse,
I holler and I whoop,
He think I happy and I is
'bout to fly the coop.

XVIII

Ole Marse, he had stud nigger,
Dat nigger hit de lick!
Ole Missus heard about him
And now she big as tick.

XIX

I put spiders in the pot,
Black widows to be sho'
They et and praise me highly,
I'se glad to see them go.

XX

I goes up to the big house
Before Ole Missus rise,
I stand right over Missus' bed
And catch her by surprise.

I say, "Git up, you lazy thing,
Git up and cook for me."
She buck her eyes 'til they pop out,
So scared she cannot see.

I tell her, "You no mo' Miss Anne,
To me you plain old Annie.
Call me Miss Lue and do it quick
Or else I whip your fannie."

She say, "I'm white and I can't cook,
My white lips can't say Miss."
I say "I slap you side your head—
Now you take that and this!"

Here come Ole Marse from other room,
"Miss Lue, if what I see
Is that you slap old Annie's face,
Hit one more lick for me."

XXI

Saint Peter tell me watch his gate,
Don't let no bad 'uns in,
And so I put my hands on hips
To stop each one that sin.

I see Ole Marsa treckin' 'long,
He trudgin' up the line,
And so I says unto myself,
At last your meat is mine.

He at the gate, he see me there,
He rear way back and swell,
I slam that gate and say to him,
"You git the hell to hell!"

XXII

Everyone done told a tale,
The last tale fall on me,
I got no right talking here
'cause y'all know I'se free.

I sho' don't chop no cotton
And I don't pick none too,
Marsa is so scared of me
I is the "Booger Boo."

I goes this way and that way
And never need no pass,
Ole Marse look down, cap in hand,
He know he bet' not sass.

Marse a lush head son of a gun,
I just now caught him plastered.
Go on y'all, lay in the shade,
'cause I done kilt the bastard.

I Been There

My body is weak and sickly
But it done served Marse well,
I'se gonna land in heaven,
Already been through hell.

Good Masters

No matter what folks say,
My Marse was kind to me,
Kind enough to up and die
And that's what set me free.

Runaway

I run away from beatin'
And just can't understan'
Why a slave that git beat too
Can tell on other man.

I'se skulkin' in the bushes
And climb up in a tree,
I know a slave done told Marse
'zackly where I be.

I'se hungry and done got weak,
Cone pone would be a feast.
It am a shame Marse stalkin' me,
He am the one the beast.

Mystery

One thing sure do shock me,
I seen Marse on his knees.
They say Ole Marse was praying,
Explain that if you please.

Shepherd

Folks think I talking to myself,
I talking to my God
'bout if the devil come too close
To poke him with His rod.

Hallelujah

I'm gonna shout, oh yes I am,
And jump up straight and down,
Back away, get a running start
When God hold up my crown

Mother and Child

Every night I dream about
Ole Marse selling my child,
I scream and holler in my sleep,
They claim that I am wild.

Don't know where she is today,
My baby was just three.
What kind of mamma would I be
If it don't worry me.

Call me crazy, call me touched,
And you can say I'm wild,
But remember it all started
When Marsa sold my child.

Sundown

The sun's goin' down, heavenly Lord,
And I go right behind it.
Cover my track, heavenly Lord,
And Ole Marse never find it.

Hezekiah

I rec'lect the driver man
Was sleeping very sound.
That's when I snuck up on him,
Now he am in the ground.

Ole Marse never caught me
But he was in a huff.
That is all, for that is that—
Fetch me my box of snuff.

Jenny

Ole Missus were a sorry sight,
She knowed that I knowed too,
Ole Marsa ran from shack to shack
Like all Ole Marsas do.

Rebel

I break the hoe, I break the plow
And here he come, that hellion.
I say right then unto myself,
This a one-man rebellion.

I stand foursquare and face Ole Marse,
He call me crazy nigger,
I rush him and I take his gun
And then I pull the trigger.

My time is come and I don't care
If they hang me from a tree,
By bein' crazy like a fox
I sent Marse 'head of me.

Mose

He bowed and scraped and loved Ole Marse,
A grovelin' black slave nigger,
And after pizenin' Ole Marse
A shufflin' black grave digger.

Scars and Stripes

I seen 'em whipped and branded too,
And strung up in the trees,
I seen a-many baby sold,
Ole Marse do what he please.

My head is full of Marsa's scars,
My back is full of stripes,
And I am even branded too,
But I wiped out my gripes.

I took my chance and grabbed his gun
And held it very steady,
Blowed off his head, I got to run—
They look for me already.

Remember

The doctor say Marse' mind is sound,
That it is wide awake,
And say when Marsa draw last breath
Then that will free old Jake.

So everything am settled now,
The lawyer heard 'im too,
But I hear something else speak out:
Say, Jake, what you gon' do?

You sho' has been good servant,
You served for thirty years,
You 'member when he sold your child
And you was full of tears?

Sissy

I won't let Marsa pat me jes'
Because I'm big and plump.
Ole Missus, she is straight up down,
Ain't nowhere is a bump.

Marse shake the sheet to find her
To see if she in bed,
She there alright, but she don't move,
She stiff jes' like she dead.

Taking Sides

Ole Marse look at de pallet,
Say "Lucius, 'member me?
Look, Lucius, at your Marsa,
You live, I set you free."

Old Lucius say, "My eyes is dim,
I know it's Marsa's voice,
But death don't lie when he am come,
I make old death my choice."

Rebuked

Y'all talkin' crazy when yer ask
A man like me that's black
Why I let Marsa beat me
And put marks on my back.

I was not scared, the point I make,
You see, I was not free,
No more than one o' Marsa's mules,
Don't be so hard on me.

Old King Cotton

Oh yeah, I know they call you King
And how you make their pockets ring,
You've really been a trying thing,
Old King Cotton,

You saw me up and down the row
Chopping grass with sharpened hoe,
Pulling weeds to help you grow,
Old King Cotton,

You saw my old black woman too
And all the things she did for you,
You saw our chillun scamper through,
Old King Cotton,

You saw them melons on the vine,
Saw me bust one many a time
And pass a chunk on down the line,
Old King Cotton,

You know that old grey mule, I bet,
How he would balk and I would fret,
But plowed until the sun did set,
Old King Cotton,

You saw me when I laid you by
And looked you over with my eye,
I said you'd bring a price that's high,
Old King Cotton,

We gonna start you ginning through,
Bless my soul, you'll see that too,
And you will hear me say to you,
Rotten, rotten cotton.

Supper Time

He swore that he would not be whipped
Or trot at beck and call,
Ole Marsa screamed, "I'll break you in,
I'll beat you 'til you crawl."

He grabbed Ole Marsa by the neck
And headed for the well
And jumping in he hollered back,
"Me an' Ole Marse eat supper in hell!"

Selling Melvina

"What bid do I hear for this comely wench?
You have seen her buttocks and bust.
She's as ripe as the fallen fruit, you see.
What do I hear? Bid on your lust."

"Five hundred I bid for that black heifer."
"By Jove, I will make it seven.
I have got to own that nigger wench,
I swear by Hell and all Heaven."

Melvina was chewing a poison leaf
And stood like a statue of stone,
The auctioneer called, "Going, going. . .
She's toppled — Hell! She's gone."

Upstart

Young Marse, you come to beat me
And say don't give no lip,
But I can't work cause rheumatiz
Is got me in the hip.

Last lickin like to kilt me,
I waits for God right now,
Tha's why I has to speak my mind
Tho' you beat me anyhow.

Ole Missus made me nurse you first,
Then my black breast stopped givin',
My baby died, you got the milk,
One reason you is livin'.

Religion

He pray, he sing, he shout and cry
And that am every Sunday,
Next thing we know, Marse whippin' us
And that am every Monday.

Duke

Marse shot the ground around his feet
To make him jig and leap,
But now he jig on Marsa's grave
So glad Marse six foot deep.

Sally

She clear her throat and spit in soup
And do it three, four time.
She throw some okra in the pot,
That too will make a slime.

Ole Marsa slop it up like hog:
"Sally, by jove, it's good!"
And Sally say, "I sure is glad,
I done the best I could."

Tom

I lay my head on choppin' block,
To Marsa I is true.
To all the niggers call me Tom,
Ole Marse is white, is you?

I hold his hat, his walkin' stick
And help him wid his coat,
And when I sin he slap my back
And say, "You doggone goat!"

I like to git that praise from Marse,
His praise is mighty slim,
And when he call me doggone goat
That's pet name come from him.

I slink around and tell Ole Marse
The secrets of the niggers,
And when I tell he kick me well,
I don't know how that figgers.

I flunky 'round and serves him
His brandy and his gin,
And when I do he take his cane
And whack me on the shin.

I look at him, I'se grinnin',
He look at me rat grim,
He knows I is good nigger,
Tell me, wha's wrong wid him?

Southern Belle

Ole Missus is a vile one,
Got everything, she rich!
But walk around house niggers
Buck naked, not a stitch.

I don't know what she provin',
Ole Marsa love the shacks,
There's something in them quarters
That his Ole Missus lacks.

Leora

They say they can't control me
And say I never happy.
How can I be when I know he,
Ole Marsa, is my pappy.

Jane

'scuse me, white folks, I'se old and dull,
Two things I does remember,
My name is Jane, I chopped Ole Marse,
I think it in December

Pete

Ole Marsa's wife done run away,
She leave him all a-sudden,
He mad as hell 'cause he done looked
And he can't find nare nudden.

Beulah

Ole Marse, he throw me on the bed
And so I fights, 'cause I is scared,
I kicks him where his trouble is,
Mine's alright, he nursin' his.

Family or Freedom

To get my freedom I would chance my life,
But I ain't running and leaving my wife.
I had a chance just yesterday,
Could have been gone far away.

Ole Marse was drunk and the driver man too,
Neither was watching as they always do.
But I'll stick out this lowly life,
I ain't running and leaving my wife.

Posted

I

Two mules for sale and one black boy,
He's strong and very big,
Now if you buy the lot of them
I'll throw in one fat pig.

II

I'm overloaded, got too much,
Niggers, chickens, hogs, and such,
Donkeys, mules, turkeys too,
This is the sale I offer you.

III

Tacked on a tree a great big sign,
"Looking for a sire?
Come and see this burly black
I have got for hire."

IV

Look out for Carrie, she's not fat,
Just showing what she's done,
So if you find her rush her back,
Reward is one for one.

V

Catch young Lindy, she looks like white,
But just another black,
Talks real smart, calls me "Damn Pa"
They say, behind my back.

VI

A black boy, George, 'bout twenty-five,
A rascal, scoundrel too,
He runs away 'bout once a month,
So I am warning you

He is a dangerous nigger,
The kind you just can't case,
He holds his cap and keeps a grin
That spreads across his face.

VII

Don't judge my nigger by his mouth,
He's young and he is stout,
The reason that he lost some teeth
Is 'cause I knocked 'em out.

VIII

Ole Lonnie is a runaway.
I greased him up real good
And put some polish on his head
To sell him if I could.

You catch that nigger, wash his head
To see if it is gray,
You know right then he is my boy—
Don't let him get away.

Telling It All

So much I hates 'bout slavery time,
Some things I hasn't tell,
But now I know Old Marse is dead
And burnin' down in hell.

Come creepin' in my cabin,
Done sold my man away,
And fumble 'round half 'o de night
And sneak out just 'fore day.

Ole Missus 'tend she do not know,
Head up and dressed up fine,
One thing I know she do not know,
I fed Ole Marse strychnine.

Mandy

Ole Marse is potbelly man,
Dat man can't see de feet,
Come sidlin' up real close to me
Like he am in de heat.

He puff and blow and then he say,
"You wench, I goin' to grind it!"
I step aside and laugh at him,
I know he never find it.

Preacher Man

White preacher like a mangy dog,
Each time he turn around
The dandruff fall from off his head
And flutter to the ground.

He preach straight to the white folks,
Sometime he turn aside
And tell us slaves that's squattin' there,
"Let Marsa tan your hide."

"You take your beatin' like a slave,
Obey and don't fight back,
You know your Marsa owns you,
You know he's white, you black."

Obey, obey, that's all I hear,
So I obeyed my mind
And when the preachin' over with
I creep up close behind.

Now ain't no flaky dandruff
Come fallin' from his head
'cause he ain't standin' up no mo',
He stretched out and he dead.

Tending in the Great House

Lou had to leave her sickly child
To sit with Missus' naughty boy
Who cut many a caper
And played with every toy.

When Missus finally came home
Lou wrapped a shawl around her head,
Then went into her cabin
To find her baby dead.

Rain

Sunshine days Ole Marsa nice,
He laugh wid us and joke,
But let dere come a rainy day
Ole Marsa break his yoke.

He trot just like a bloodhound
And run from hut to cabin
To find black woman all alone
And try to start to dabbin'.

Traveling Light

Gonna knock off early Saturday night,
Walk for miles in the cool moonlight,
Get there soon 'cause my feet be light,
See my wife and be all right.

This Is It

I holler hallelujah,
I jump up and I shout,
Ain't gettin' on my knees no more,
Done just 'bout wore 'em out.

Things go 'long about the same,
I try to do what's right,
I can't please Marse and can't please God,
I reckon He is white.

I always prayed to the Lord
That things be turned about,
Ain't gettin' on my knees no more,
Done just 'bout wore 'em out.

Emancipation Proclamation

Seed Abe Lincum wid my eyes,
He travelin' through the lan',
Know what else my eyes do see?
He one mo' ugly man.

Enslaved

His only slave freed and gone,
Red-necked cracker all alone,
No crop to plant, no crop to reap,
All his troubles piled so steep.

Barefoot, ragged, hurting, sick,
Just a meat skin now to lick.
Stomach empty, tightened belt,
Hunger's for niggers, so he felt.

"Boy," he said, "you damn' old black,
Out of my sight and don't come back.
Don't want your food, out of my sight!
I'm clinging to this—I'm white, I'm white!"

Lay Me Down

My bones a-creakin' on a creaky bed,
No soft place for to lay my head,
One day good Lord gonna lay me down,
Soft, soft sleepin' under the ground.

Movin' Nowhere

I keep on movin', ain't gettin' nowhere,
Plow from here and down to there,
Start again from here to there,
I keep on movin', ain't gettin' nowhere.

Cracked Saucer

My saucer done cracked
And my coffee's gone,
Got nothin' ter wash down
The cold cone pone

Old crack so tricky
Let it leak out slow,
Didn't see my coffee
When it started to go

My saucer done cracked
My coffee done gone,
Nothin' to wash down
The cold cone pone

The Vision

I've seen heaven, children,
While lying in my bed
Golden gates flew open,
A light shined on my head

I saw angels flying
With glitter on their wings,
It almost blinded me
To see such pretty things

I've seen heaven, children,
And I'll be there for sure
On that great getting up day
Because my heart is pure

For Aubrie

His Hands

They told the story better
Than anything he could ever say.
They were a loving symbol
Of his life from day to day.

To them no man was stranger
As they gave to those in need.
They were eager to share his earnings,
Had never known the thing called greed.

They lifted heavy timber,
Worked with stone and mortar, dug clay,
Yet gently held the baby
At the close of some hard day.

They held his Bible firmly,
Turning slowly page by page.
They were devout and constant,
And never struck in rage.

They did not know the manicurist's touch
Or glisten with jewels set in rings.
They were adorned with creases and careworn,
And only dealt in honest things.

How well I know they labored
From sun-up 'til eventide.
His hands were so willing,
As if an unseen censor their guide.

The last time I saw them, may God have mercy,
They were folded across his breast.
Though Papa will live eternally,
May his hands forever rest.

Timing

Now and then she would shout in church,
Walking down the aisle,
With one hand raised toward heaven,
Screaming all the while.

She wanted to be seen
When she was all decked out,
When wearing a new dress or hat
Was the only time she'd shout.

Mourners Bench

The sinners were coaxed to sit up front.
There were gamblers and a wench,
There were whoremongers and drunkards
And backsliders on the bench.

The preacher sweated and hollered,
"He'll forgive, don't care what you do.
Just trust Him tonight, Oh trust Him,
For Jesus loves all of you."

He screamed, "Trust in Jesus,
Just listen to His teaching."
Those on the bench were saved
By his pleading and his preaching.

The wench went right back to whoring,
The gamblers went right back to gambling,
The drunkard went right back to drinking,
The whoremonger right back to rambling.

They all had one thing in common,
They felt they had nothing to fear.
They'd keep on sinning since He forgives,
And return to the bench next year.

An Egg in Each Basket

I just can't put all my trust
In a fella I ain't seen,
I don't know whether He's friendly,
I don't know whether He's mean.

Now there's that other fella,
The one they say is so bad.
If I should crack a joke for him,
Could be the best laugh he's had.

Gotta stay on the good side
Of the devil and with God,
Don't know which one I land up with
When they put me in the sod.

Old Man

Old man, you ain't always been good
And doing all the things you should,
I bet you did everything you could,
Long time ago,

Now, you ain't been good all your life,
I bet you danced to fiddle and fife
And s'peck you used to beat your wife,
Long time ago,

Now you try to give advice,
The things you say sound just too nice.
Say, didn't you used to shoot them dice,
Long time ago?

Now you've got a pious look,
Just as if you wouldn't crook.
Whose wife was it that you took,
Long time ago?

Go on, old man, and play your role,
I ain't gonna tell it to a soul,
But God done wrote it on His scroll
A long time ago.

Jackleg

"Sinners, gamblers, whores and such,
Come off from that back row,
Come to the front and tell the Lord
To make the devil go.

"Come ye brethren, come up close
And come ye sisters too.
But don't you sisters get too close,
No telling what I do."

Collection

She emptied her purse on the table
'cause the preacher had called her honey.
She went on home satisfied
Though she had no insurance money.

Feeding the Pastor

She caught a chicken and wrung its neck,
She had already cooked a roast,
But she wanted to load the table
So he could eat and boast.

The pastor came right on time
And headed for the table,
He tucked a napkin under his chin
And ate what he was able.

He drove away in a cadillac
Like so many black preachers do,
Since she was good at wringing necks
She should have wrung his too.

No Flowers

She was black and sold moonshine
For a white man she called Joe,
She was a bootleg woman,
Yeah, she was that for sho'.

She had a daughter, name of Lil,
And the night that mamma died
Lil took a swig of moonshine
And they say she never cried,
They say she never cried.

She got on the phone and talked to Joe,
"Have you heard that mamma's dead?
Bring two gallons of moonshine—
One for the foot of the casket
And one for to set at the head,
Yeah, one for the foot of the casket
And one for to set at the head."

And Joe brought the moonshine,
Two gallons, like Lil said,
One for the foot of the casket
And one for to set at the head,
Yeah, one for the foot of the casket
And one for to set at the head.

Gambler

He lived so recklessly that
His mamma told him, "Son,
If you never mend your ways
You'll die with your shoes on,
Die with your shoes on."

He kept on shooting dice
And not once did he pray,
Though seldom was he lucky
He continued anyway.

That he tried with loaded dice
The gamblers had no doubt,
He shook the dice and rolled them,
And then a shot rang out.

He screamed, "Come take off my shoes,"
Knowing that he would die,
"I wanna make mamma out
A low-down Goddamn lie,
Low-down Goddamn lie."

Let Them Come

Let them come
As they usually do by night
With eyes of blue steel
And hearts of stone,

Let them come
As they usually do in throngs
With whiskey breath and
Tobacco dripping mouths
To take one black,

Let them wait
As they usually do
Squatting on haunches
Lusting for blood,

Let them come, let them come,
Not a one would dare
Come alone.

Cannonball

I worked this strip to make the railroad track,
I grunted umph, umph, cross ties on my back,
I know the railroad and how it was built,
I know 'bout the black men the railroad kilt.

A train can't run unless it got a track.
I toted that shining steel on my back.
Yeah, I laid them ties and I drove the spike
When they started the railroad through this pike.

The train blow for the crossing, slowing down,
Don't want for to stop in this little town.
I hear them wheels going clickety clack,
It seems to me it's ridin' on my back.

I'm all bent over from toting the steel.
The train moves through like a long, long eel.
It's highballing through to hit the big town.
If you gonna ride, better flag it down.

Yeah, it pass this town like it don't exist.
I don't wave at the train, I shake my fist.
I ain't got no money and I can't ride,
But I laid them tracks and I got my pride.

Little Boys

"Little white boy, when you grow up,
What do you want to be?"
"Oh, doctor, lawyer, or president,
It is all left up to me."

"Little black boy, when you grow up,
What will you be, tell me?"
"You asking me, a little black boy?
I be plain lucky to be."

Rigmarole: Puzzles For Children

Some folks can live while others die,
Some folks can laugh while others cry,
Some places are far and some are nigh,
Some folks like cake and others pie,
There's a low for every high,
Sometimes I wonder why.

Well, there's a this for every that,
And there's a tit for every tat,
You got to sit before you've sat,
And there's a chit for every chat,
You got to spit before you've spat,
If that's not true I'll eat my hat.

If there's a criss, well there's a cross,
And something found was something lost,
Some things are free while others cost,
Some ride a mule, some ride a hoss,
A rolling stone don't catch no moss,
You work for me, that makes me boss.

Some roads are crooked, some are straight,
Some don't eat much, some clean the plate,
Some folks are early and some are late,
Some get in soon while others wait,
You call it luck, I call it fate,
You go through cracks, I find the gate.

Some folks got hair, some wear a wig,
Some dance the waltz, some do a jig,
Some things zag and some things zig,
Some are little and some are big,
Some get it easy while others dig,
I got my cow, you got your pig.

Here is rain and there is dew,
Here am I and there are you,
You are one, we both make two,
There is old and there is new,
Some things we fry and some things stew,
I don't know, I wish I knew. . .

The land is dry, the river wet,
Some babies cry and others fret,
Some folks perspire while others sweat,
Some doors are open, others shet,
I feel the wind, ain't seen it yet,
Now just how silly can this get?

There's a smile for every frown,
If I'm a fool then you're a clown,
If this is up, then that is down,
If this is square, then that is round,
Some folks swim and others drown,
I know how crazy all this sounds!

For Ella Jenkins

Daylight Saving Time

Some folks are getting mighty smart
In every kind of way,
Some Alec done got too smart
And changed the time of day.

This time has got us mesmerized,
It gets us up too soon,
And then we have to go to bed
'bout time we see the moon.

Setting all the clocks ahead,
Messing up the town,
And changing this and changing that
Done run it in the groun'.

Trying to make that sun wait—
That sun don't tell no lies,
Folks better stay in folks' place,
And quit messing with the skies.

God's gonna come riding through
And raging in his wrath,
Gonna strike down everybody
That happens in his path.

You gonna ask the Lord to wait
So you can change His mind,
And God's gonna say, "Man, I can't wait,
I come on Daylight Saving Time."

New Address

Stop sending duns to my house.
Them bills is Phillip's bills.
I told you he don't live here.
Phillip is in the hills.

He left here in November,
He ain't been back no mo',
Phillip's got a new address
Where the wild flowers grow.

His address is in a graveyard—
Which one? You look about,
I don't tell The Man
Where Phillip's hiding out.

News

Guess I'll go on down to the newsstand
And tell Isaiah Mack is dead.
Mack, who went every day to buy the paper,
Talking with Isaiah about the headlines
And the editorials and obituaries,
The ones that's gone.

Two old cronies
Who got many a laugh over the society pages,
The pictures of ladies and gentlemen
All in evening gowns and tux and ties.
Mack's death didn't make the paper,
So I'll go down and let Isaiah know
Mack won't be coming 'round no more.

For W. E. B. Du Bois

Now the fragrant petals shower downward
That hung suspended in an air of fear,
But he is gone and now they fall resplendent
In solemn reverence for that mighty seer.

That great exponent of the freedom surge
Who advocated that the black man fight,
Whose dreams transcended all our shallow hopes
And set a fuse exploding into light.

Our cross lay like a millstone on his heart.
We let him bear the burden all alone.
Now we come forward eloquent with praise,
Our silence broken after he is gone.

Too late! But not too late to change our lot,
To re-evaluate the Negro's gains,
To call together twenty million men
And break the lock that holds us now in chains.

For now we see the fierceness of his truth,
A history of cruelty to our race.
It shall be changed if written with our blood.
His name will be a sign to mark the place.

Oh, Africa! Be gentle to his mound,
For tender is your bosom for your own,
Dark are your nights but filled with stars of hope
That we shall reap the harvest he has sown.

Flight

The dusk comes quietly in
Soon to make way for the night,
The night grows darker and darker,
And is lost in the dawn of light.

Uncertainty

You are two-faced but comrade you are fair.
No one can be certain or foresee,
For those who weep at morn at eve may laugh,
Who live today tomorrow may not be.

You stay on until death steps in,
With fleeting feet you then take flight,
You know death has power over you
As daybreak has power over night.

Then you are gone to plague
Some new-born infant at its mother's breast,
To cling until the final breath is drawn
And that poor soul has lost itself in rest.

As I await the uninvited guest
And you are fading from the darkening room,
I will honor death's command
With growing certainty in my gloom.

I may not see the tears but hear the sobbing
And realize those gathered there are grieving,
But if you stay I'll not know why they weep,
Because I lived or because I'm leaving.

Shadows in the Light

i
The dose of life is fatal in itself.
Beginning indicates there is an end.
The leaves of spring sing many happy songs
But finally are caught in autumn's wind.

At dawn I heralded the newborn day,
At noon I realized it was growing,
When evening came I saw it stooped with age
And as I slept it passed without my knowing.

How often have I watched that night balloon
Shining veiled behind a drifting cloud,
And seen the sun with all its beams of light
Drop suddenly behind an evening shroud.

A rainbow disappearing as you gaze,
A bubble blown and touched and then no more.
Birth and death do not astound this world,
And oceans keep on rolling, dip or pour.

ii
Expect a big return for little spent
While each and everyone feels duty bound?
The Sower really can't expect to reap
From seed that He let fall on stony ground.

iii

Forgotten, now the markers gather moss,
Not one has had a visitor today,
For those who grieved and wept upon the ground
Have dried their tears and gone along their way.

They're balanced, with everything precise —
The millionaire and beggar weigh the same.
The scales were standing still when they went out.
They went as empty-handed as they came.

That same revolving door that whirled them in
Kept turning and has whirled them once again
Into a world of nothingness.
Who knows but that their entry was in vain.

For life is as the lonely blind who reach
And never find the object of the search,
The bird that fills the air with its sweet song
That falls on deaf ears underneath its perch.

Whirl on you tipsy topsy-turvy man,
Keep spinning on, but He who strung the top
Looks down and watches every round you make
And knows when you will wobble, tilt and stop.

It's He who rings the silken curtain down,
No matter how spectacular the show.
Performance done, rewarded? Who can say,
When no one has returned to let us know.

They are worn out and wrecked beyond repair.
The motor stopped that stopped on all the others.
And so the great machine that we call man
Is carted off and junked beside his brothers.

Trumpet

Heaven, ready for reunion
Golden goblets for communion
All the angels now are singing
Music from each harp is ringing
Every scroll is now unrolling
Every bell in Heaven tolling
Sting of death has lost its power
Now has come the greatest hour
Gabriel takes the trumpet.

On the world the dawn is breaking
When there comes an awful quaking
Now the land has started sliding
Sinners look around for hiding
Just as they are bent on fleeing
Dumb are speaking, blind are seeing
As the trumpet's notes are nearing
All the deaf have started hearing
Gabriel, blow the trumpet.

Gabriel, tense with temples pounding,
Gabriel with the trumpet sounding
Mountains now have started skipping
And the moon has started dripping
Sun and stars are now retreating
Trumpet's echoes now repeating
Every wind has started blowing
Every stream increased its flowing
As Gabriel blows the trumpet.

Seas and oceans start their churning
Belching up, their dead returning
Claps of thunder, lightning flashing
Waves against the rocks are dashing
Time has stopped, time is standing
Humble to His great commanding
Clouds are bursting, rain is pounding
All the while the doomsday sounding
Of Gabriel at the trumpet.

Those in Christ are first emerging
Soon the graves will start their purging
Rhyming with the thunder's clapping
Every shroud has started flapping
All the saints begin their shouting
Not a one of them is doubting
Every one of them rejoicing
Everyone His praises voicing
Awakened by the trumpet.

Assembling now the saints are singing
Suddenly like birds when winging
Into Heaven now ascending
Multitudes of them are wending
Some uplifted in a twinkling
By surprise, they had no inkling
Saints are going, going, going
Lifted up by soft winds blowing
Blowing with the trumpet.

Just as all the saints are leaving
Tombs and graves have started heaving
Out the sinners come a-tumbling
Now the thunder's really rumbling
Darkness on the world is creeping
Sinners screaming, sinners weeping
The world is off its axis, reeling
Sinners crying, sinners squealing
Are heard above the trumpet.

Rocks are every exit blocking
Jaws of hell are now unlocking
Earth is crumbling, earth is splitting
And all hell has started spitting
Spitting fumes that start one choking
Sinners now are scorching, smoking
Terror, gripping and appalling
Every sinner, falling, falling
As Gabriel sounds the trumpet.

The hungry mouth of hell is gapping
Flames are licking, flames are lapping
Every wheel in hell is turning
Everything in hell is burning
Everyone in hell is sprawling
Every voice in hell is squalling
To escape is just a notion
For hell is in perpetual motion
Set off by the trumpet.

For Vivian E. Johnson Cook

Elma Stuckey is the granddaughter of former slaves. Born in Memphis in 1907, she came to Chicago with her husband and two children in 1945. She has worked as hat check girl, maid, rural school teacher, head nursery school teacher, and supervisor for the Illinois Department of Labor. Her poems have been enthusiastically received, by white and black, at such colleges and universities as Harvard, Wisconsin, and Malcolm X, as well as at high schools and community organizations. She is the mother of Sterling Stuckey, the distinguished young historian and author at Northwestern University, and of Delois Jean Morrison, a Chicago schoolteacher.